Face to Face with Karma:

Your Guide to Fate and the Grand Law of Karma

To all the seekers of truth: may your hearts
be ever-ignited by the flame of love.

Face to Face with Karma:

Your Guide to Fate and the Grand Law of Karma

Dr Ric Neo

MANTRA BOOKS

London, UK
Washington, DC, USA

CollectiveInk

First published by Mantra Books, 2025
Mantra Books is an imprint of Collective Ink Ltd.,
Unit 11, Shepperton House, 89 Shepperton Road, London, N1 3DF
office@collectiveinkbooks.com
www.collectiveinkbooks.com
www.mantra-books.net

For distributor details and how to order please visit the 'Ordering' section on our website.

ISBN: 978 1 80341 900 8
978 1 80341 922 0 (ebook)
Library of Congress Control Number: 2024920161

A CIP catalogue record for this book is available from the British Library.

Design: Lapiz Digital Services

UK: Printed and bound by CPI Group (UK) Ltd, Croydon, CR0 4YY
Printed in North America by CPI GPS partners

Contents

Preface

This book was born from a series of profound visions I received over the past year. The first one came during my maiden plant medicine journey, and the subsequent ones during further spiritual retreats and meditative encounters. A common thread and recurrent figure across these visions was the Lord of Karma.

My initial encounter with the Lord of Karma was excruciating. I was made to witness a relentless unveiling of the karmic process — how karmic bonds were energetically forged and wound between souls bound to each other. I saw how these knots were crystallized in blood and were given very stark, visual impressions of pain, flesh, spiritual essence, blood and bone.

As those who have experienced visions know, the scariest aspect about them is how they take place entirely in your mind — a place we cannot run away and escape from, unlike in the physical world. We simply have to surrender to the whole experience, no matter how scary, disturbing or painful.

Aside from seeing the energetic formation of karma, the next few visions led me to sit through judgments of my entire life thus far. I was never a manipulative or malevolent person, but I was walked through even the most minute details — such as taking an extra dollar when I was a child — all of it I felt great shame for. Ironically, the energy from the Lord of Karma was not one of judgment but that of a compassionate elder, and it is, in fact, my own self who casts these judgments and feels the embarrassment.

It was also reiterated to me constantly that in my position as a spiritual wayshower, all who come to me wholly place not just their trust but their lives in my hands — and with this great power comes great responsibility. I am not to fail them.

Subsequent visions with the Lord of Karma eventually became much lighter, and in my most recent one I was told that I have unwound the bulk of my karmic debt.

This book is thus born out of these most recent encounters with the Lord of Karma, in addition to over a decade of spiritual work, service and scholarship. It is my intention that the teachings of this book provide the keys that people can use to free themselves from the cycle of Samsara – should it be their intention to do so.

May the Loving Light of our Creator guide you Home
Dr Ric Neo

One of the author's karmic visions.

Chapter 1

Introduction

This book will give you a crystal-clear and the **most spiritually complete** understanding of the greatest fundamental law governing our existence both on Earth and beyond: the Grand Law of Karma. It is drawn from a number of visions I received throughout 2023 and 2024 that brought me face to face with the Lord of Karma himself, in addition to over a decade of spiritual work, service and scholarship.

Even though we cannot perceive it in an obvious way, karma exists as a universal law and is very real. **I repeat — karma is very real**, and it works as consistently as the other governing laws on Earth such as gravity. In fact, karma is infallible and far more reliable than these other lesser laws. As the Christed one said in Luke 12:7: "Indeed, the very hairs of your head are all numbered."

As one of the most fundamental and universal laws of the cosmos, echoes of this Grand Law are found in religions, philosophies, and spiritual systems across the world, and spanning thousands and thousands of years. Its prevalence is a testament to not just its importance, especially on Earth, but also to the unyielding, repeated and loving attempts by Enlightened Ones to provide guidance to us on Earth.

We will begin this book with a broad overview here. **What exactly is karma and how does it work?**

Karma is not at all a crude system of punishment or reward. Instead, at its core, karma is the universal principle of cause and effect that governs every single thing each of us can do. As Creator beings, every deed, every word, and every thought we release into the world creates ripples, both immediate and far-reaching. These ripples, in turn, shape not only our present experiences but also influence the possibilities of our futures. Karma thus refers to the dynamics of cause & effect — in the simplest terms, **what are the consequences of one's deeds (every single one of them)? How do these deeds affect others, and thus cycle back to the person**?

Within the Law of Karma lies the greatest opportunity for each one of us to become self-aware — to awaken, and to be conscious. **To be conscious of what, you may ask**. It is to be conscious of that which you are creating at each PRESENT moment, as a divine spark of God. Are you aware of the consequences of that which you are creating? Or as spiritual initiates like to ask: **Are you *awake***?

Thus, to understand the Grand Law of Karma is to gain a compass for navigating life's challenges and recognizing the hidden forces behind the events that take place in our lives. Karma empowers us, reminding us that even within complex circumstances, we are always in control. We become conscious architects of our destiny, taking responsibility for the choices we make.

Karma is neither fatalistic nor deterministic. It is not an unchangeable "fate" or "destiny" that a God far away has planned for us. Instead, the law emphasizes the responsibility we each bear for our own life conditions — and more importantly, it highlights the potential for growth and change within every moment. Yes, the past casts its long shadows; undoubtedly, many of us on Earth are still living out and balancing the karma of poor choices made in previous lifetimes. Yet, the future remains malleable and truly infinite, shaped by our present intentions and actions.

How, then, are we to overcome the dynamics of karma? The best guidance that can be given to this is that we accept our current, difficult conditions as "the cross that we shall bear" (Luke 14:27). They have arisen because of past actions we took, and by experiencing them we unwind the karmic energies that are attached to our souls. Yet, we can commit to making better decisions in our current lives. By loving, accepting and forgiving more, we definitively create the conditions for future positivity and ease.

In this book we begin by first traversing historical and spiritual landscapes, exploring karma's roots in ancient spiritual traditions like Hinduism and Buddhism. We'll examine its origins, diverse interpretations and unpack the core principles that guide this Grand Universal Law.

Next, we delve into the 8 Laws of Karma that explore the intricacies and dynamics of karma, including the purpose of karma, the different types of karma, and various considerations as well as methods to alleviate karmic debt. Through this, we will gain a ***crystal-clear*** understanding of how karma operates not just on an individual scale but also collectively within the vast interconnected web of existence.

One final word on this book's presentation. The writings are presented in a deliberately succinct and direct manner. Coming from an academic background, I have seen how complex writing styles serve not only to confuse readers, but also to deliberately obfuscate (or hide) important knowledge and wisdom from the general public. Too long has such an important Grand Universal Law been kept hidden and obscured from the people. My sole intention here is the opposite — this book aims to bring the light of divine wisdom to all. For ***"Ye are gods; and all of you are children of the most High"*** (Psalm 82:6).

Chapter 2

Unpacking Karma

Karma is drawn from the Sanskrit word *kármán,* meaning "action" or "deed." It refers to the principle that every action has a consequence, either positive or negative, depending on the nature and intention of the action. Karma is linked to the concept of personal responsibility and virtuous behavior. By acting in a righteous manner and cultivating positive thoughts and intentions, one creates good karma and experiences positive consequences in the future. On the flipside, negative actions and intentions will result in negative consequences.

What are some examples of actions that generate karma?

- Causing harm or injury to others, either physically or emotionally.
- Killing.
- Stealing, cheating, or taking what is not freely given.
- Lying, deceiving others.
- Divisive speech, gossiping or slandering others.
- Harsh, abusive or hurtful speech.
- Harboring ill-will, resentment, or wishing harm on others.
- More complex karmic dynamics also exist. For example, by spreading a false teaching and having others lead their lives erroneously because of this.

We tend to perceive this cause-and-effect chain as separated in time due to the way we perceive time. But as viewed from a higher reality, the cause and the effect are not separated but are entirely one. Indeed, the karmic consequences of ALL actions are immediately generated when an action is taken. **When we punch the wall, do we not immediately feel pain**?

Thus, when we hurt someone, the counterbalancing consequences of us being hurt in turn will inevitably be immediately generated for us to experience in the future. The delay that we see between any cause and its effect on our lives is merely a characteristic of third dimensional reality, where time is perceived by our consciousness as linear for the purpose of experience and growth.

Karma mandates that all freely undertaken actions which bring pain or harm to another being of any kind in the universe incur an energetic "debt" which must be met and set aside through equivalent experience in a phase of existence on the part of the individual responsible for that action. For example, by being viciously hateful towards a minority community, you will be required to experience the flipside – which can manifest as you taking a subsequent incarnation as the minority you victimized. This Grand Law is imposed by the Great Architects of the Universe as part of the cosmic scheme of salvation (which simply means growth) for all souls and cannot be avoided or annulled by any action on the part of any being, whether in physical form or in a higher form.

The Golden Rule

Karma is also called the Golden Rule and it is found across all of humanity's great religious and spiritual traditions:

New Testament: "Do not be deceived, God is not mocked; for whatever a man sows, that he will also reap." — Galatians 6:7
This verse is attributed to the Apostle Paul, who wrote the Epistle to the Galatians. Paul's writings were deeply influenced

by early Christian teachings and his own experiences, and they often emphasize themes of divine justice and moral causation. While the principle of sowing and reaping reflects broader spiritual traditions, Paul's articulation of this concept serves to align ethical conduct with the divine order.

Hindu Vedas: "No one who does good work will ever come to a bad end, either here or in the world to come." — Bhagavad Gita
From ancient Vedic traditions, this teaching reflects the Law of Karma and the eternal cycle of rebirth and spiritual progression. The *Vedas*, some of the oldest spiritual texts, detail how righteous actions accumulate positive energy that influences future lifetimes. Living ethically aligns the individual with the cosmic order (Rta), promoting spiritual liberation and unity with the divine.

Islamic Quran: "The recompense will always fit the nature of the act." — Surah An-Nahl 16:126
The *Quran*, the holy book of Islam, was revealed to Muhammad through the archangel Gabriel over approximately 23 years. The principle of divine justice and the precise balance of actions and their consequences, as emphasized in this verse, has been further explored and developed by early Islamic scholars and Sufi mystics.

Buddhism: "Hurt not others in ways that you yourself would find hurtful." — Udana-Varga 5:18
This teaching is rooted in ancient Indian spiritual traditions and was systematized by the Buddha, who emphasized the interconnectedness of all life. The principle reflects the Law of Karma and the importance of ethical conduct in breaking free from the cycle of Samsara. Compassionate actions purify the mind and elevate the soul, facilitating the path to enlightenment.

Confucianism: "Do not do unto others what you would not have them do unto you." — The Analects 15:23
Originating from ancient Chinese philosophy, this teaching reflects the principle of Ren (benevolence) and the cosmic order emphasized in Daoist thought. Confucius integrated these ideas into a moral framework that promotes social harmony and spiritual integrity.

Ancient Egypt: "Do not do to anyone what is hateful to you." — Tale of the Eloquent Peasant
This stems from the ancient Egyptian concept of Ma'at, the divine order and balance upheld by the goddess Ma'at. Priests believed that living in accordance with Ma'at ensured harmony in both the earthly and spiritual realms. Ethical integrity aligns the soul with the divine order, securing a favorable judgment in the afterlife and maintaining cosmic equilibrium.

Zoroastrianism: "That nature alone is good which refrains from doing unto another whatsoever is not good for itself." — Dadistan-i-dinik 94:5
This reflects the dualistic nature of Zoroastrian cosmology, emphasizing the struggle between Ahura Mazda (light) and Angra Mainyu (darkness). Zoroastrian priests taught that ethical actions align individuals with the divine order (Asha), contributing to the cosmic battle against chaos. Virtuous behavior strengthens the soul's light, aiding in the ultimate triumph of good over evil.

Taoism: "Regard your neighbor's gain as your gain, and your neighbor's loss as your own loss." — T'ai Shang Kan Ying P'ien
This teaching originates from Taoist philosophy, which emphasizes the interconnectedness of all life. Laozi and other Taoist sages taught that empathy and compassion align individuals with the natural flow of the universe (the Tao).

Jainism: "In happiness and suffering, in joy and grief, we should regard all creatures as we regard our own self." — Lord Mahavir 24th Tirthankara
This principle emphasizes ahimsa (non-violence) and the interconnectedness of all souls. Lord Mahavir's teachings highlight the importance of compassion and ethical conduct in purifying karma and elevating the soul. Recognizing the divinity in all beings fosters spiritual growth and alignment with the universal consciousness.

Judaism: "What is hateful to you, do not do to your fellow. That is the entire Torah, and the rest is commentary." — Talmud, Shabbat 31a
This has roots in ancient Semitic traditions and was further developed by Jewish mystics and scholars. Kabbalistic thought interprets this principle as essential for Tikkun Olam (repairing the world) and aligning with divine will. Righteous actions elevate the soul and contribute to the spiritual restoration of the universe.

Native American (Lakota): "Do not wrong or hate your neighbor. For it is not he who you wrong, but yourself." — Lakota Principle
Drawn from Native American spirituality, this principle emphasizes the interconnectedness of all life and the sacred unity of existence. Lakota shamans taught that harming others disrupts the balance of the natural and spiritual worlds.

Wicca: "An ye harm none, do what ye will." — The Wiccan Rede
This teaching originates from ancient pagan traditions and was systematized in modern Wicca by modern practitioners. It emphasizes the ethical use of magical practices and personal responsibility, reflecting the interconnectedness of all actions.

Scientific Lens

From the scientific perspective, karma is precisely what Newton's Third Law — theory of cause and effect — refers to. Newton's Third Law is a cornerstone of classical mechanics which states that "for every action, there is an equal and opposite reaction." This speaks to the dynamic balance within our physical universe. Whether it's the recoil of a gun, the explosive force of a rocket or theft against our neighbor, every exerted force is met with a counterforce. Translating this into the realm of karma shows an identical mirroring dynamic operating within the fabric of existence. Every action, every intention, every ripple of energy we release sets in motion forces that must ultimately find balance and equilibrium.

Inertia, another scientific principle, also reflects the workings of karma. The principle of inertia explains that an object at rest will stay at rest until acted upon, and an object in motion remains in motion unless influenced by an external force. In this similar vein, our actions, thoughts, and energetic imprints gain a momentum of their own. This momentum doesn't simply dissipate, but rather continues to linger until it's counterbalanced or transformed. This cycle of actions setting off equal and opposite reactions can be seen as the karmic mechanism propelling us through experiences.

Finally, according to the first Law of Thermodynamics known as the Law of Conservation of Energy, energy can only be converted from one form to another; it cannot be created or destroyed. This, again, greatly elucidates the Grand Law of Karma. Our actions do not vanish — they shape the conditions for equivalent experiences to eventually manifest in our lives. This inherent universal law ensures that every action, thought and vibration ultimately finds its balancing point.

Thus, karma is not about punishment, reward or determinism, but represents a complex interplay where free will and unforeseen forces meet within the grand dance of existence. **It is the Law of CONSEQUENCE, and not punishment**. Each incarnation, from this perspective, is an opportunity to both resolve past karmic reverberations and set new, hopefully positive ones in motion. This continues in perpetuality until our souls achieve enlightenment and return to our Creator.

A Framework for Growth

For our souls in search of variety of experience and spiritual growth, the universe thus becomes a cosmic classroom. Each action, each encounter, provides a different energetic signature to be countered and eventually balanced. Just as a scientist might conduct a series of experiments with different parameters to understand a phenomenon, the Grand Law of Karma allows the soul to experience the full spectrum of encounters and consequences, expanding its awareness and capacity. Even if a soul should choose to inflict pain on another, it is not judged as "wrong." **It is merely a decision to experience BOTH aspects of the scenario, gaining great wisdom and expanding the soul's consciousness in the process**. Challenges faced in this life are nothing more than echoes of past actions seeking resolution — opportunities to respond differently, break old patterns, and generate a new energetic momentum.

The importance of consciousness and self-awareness cannot be overstated. It's not enough to simply change physical outside behavior if our deep-seated, emotional motives, biases and thought patterns remain unaddressed. To unpack the hidden forces behind our behavior and other observable external conditions, we must delve into our inner worlds, examining the intentions behind our actions and becoming **conscious** of ***how we think and why do we so***, which collectively set off energies in motion. This reflection is crucial for successfully navigating the karmic currents with awareness and creating lasting transformation.

Recall that experiences don't end with a single lifetime, but rather, the soul carries the karmic echo of past actions and tendencies as it embarks on new incarnations. This offers a broader context for understanding why individuals are born into vastly different circumstances — why certain people die young (perhaps it is a Master Soul choosing a short incarnation to help raise awareness of poverty), why some are born with disabilities (perhaps a challenge to himself to rise above it) or is a victim of abuse (balancing of past debt). There is an infinite number of cosmic curriculums tailored to address the unique karmic patterns of different souls and to facilitate further growth.

Balancing of Energies

It is important to understand that karma is balanced in a multi-dimensional way. Actions on the physical plane leave repercussions also in the emotional, mental, and spiritual realms. When we act from a place of greed, for example, the "equal and opposite reaction" may manifest as an experience of lack, perhaps in the material sense where we might experience financial losses in the stock market — or perhaps as an emotional emptiness within. This mirroring serves as a learning mechanism, pushing us towards growth and the embodiment of higher qualities.

Karma casts a wide net over our actions, encompassing not just deeds but also the subtler realm of thoughts and intentions. Imagine an angry outburst, charged with negativity. While the physical expression of anger may eventually subside, its energetic imprint lingers within our field and attracts experiences that resonate with that initial anger until that energy is balanced. This can, for example, draw an incident in which someone gets angry at you, giving you the experience of being on the receiving end of an angry outburst in turn. Even if unspoken, the very intention towards harm generates a ripple in the field, setting off its own karmic trajectory.

Remember again that karma is not a punishment or a reward, but simply a cosmic, impartial law — the manifestation of divine free will.

Thou shalt do as thou please but thou shalt get the consequences of thine choices.

Indeed, everyone always gets exactly what they are creating. That's the point of free will and karma. Every action, every intention, casts a ripple in the universal pond, eventually returning to us in unexpected ways. It's not always a direct one-to-one identical correspondence, but the interconnectedness of the universe ensures that no act goes unnoticed, no choice unacknowledged.

Chapter 3

Historical Origins

The concept of karma has its roots in ancient Indian spiritual traditions that predate organized religion. Its origins are linked to the earliest rise of Hinduism, Buddhism, and Jainism, where karma became a foundational principle explaining the cycles of existence, righteousness, and the quest for liberation from suffering.

Within the Vedic scriptures, dating back to approximately 1500–500 BCE, the earliest mentions of karma described the concept not as a rigid system of punishment and reward, but rather a natural law of action and consequence. The hymns of the Rigveda discussed "Ṛta," a cosmic order where actions had inherent repercussions shaping the balance of the universe. It states: ***"According as one acts, according as one conducts himself, so does he become. The doer of good becomes good. The doer of evil becomes evil. One becomes virtuous by virtuous action, bad by bad action."*** This idea of cosmic causality laid the groundwork for the more complex understandings of karma that would follow.

The *Upanishads,* mystical texts composed between 800–500 BCE, deepened the exploration of karma. It was in these texts that karma became inextricably linked with reincarnation. The *Upanishads* taught that the soul is eternal and that it transmigrates from one body to another according to its karma. One's actions, intentions, and the accumulated weight of past lives determined not only their present circumstances but also sowed the seeds of their future births. Karma, therefore, became the governing force propelling the soul through countless existences on the wheel of Samsara, or reincarnation.

The Purpose of Suffering

The *Vedas* also prescribed various rites that are meant to appease the gods, who are thought to be the dispensers of karma. For example, the *Yajurveda* says: "By sacrifice the gods bestow all blessings. Sacrifice is the navel of the universe. Sacrifice is the bridge to the immortal. Sacrifice is the support of all creatures."

The *Yajurveda* points not to simplistic ritualistic offering but to a more profound principle of exchange and the maintenance of cosmic balance. By offering sacrifices, one seeks positive blessings, forgiveness for transgressions, and the mitigation of negative karmic repercussions. Yajna, therefore, is used to maintain harmony within the universe, ensuring blessings and a smooth karmic cycle of cause and consequence.

In this way, ***suffering represents a conceptual counterbalance to past negative actions that can help restore a sense of cosmic equilibrium***. Even when seemingly random, suffering can serve a greater purpose within a complex divine plan beyond our immediate understanding. Importantly, suffering is a catalyst for spiritual growth when embraced with awareness. Experiencing hardships can foster empathy, humility, a deeper appreciation of life's impermanence, and motivate a soul towards actions that align with higher principles.

Nonetheless, attempts to influence the intensity and nature of the karmic experiences we face — or "burn off" negative karma — through willfully seeking suffering are misguided and counterproductive. Self-flagellation or actively courting hardship reflects an ego-driven desire to control or manipulate the karmic process. True spiritual growth requires a surrender to the flow of life, trusting that if suffering is necessary for our evolution, the universe will provide the appropriate experiences without us needing to force the issue.

Ultimately, there is no way to escape karma. While it involves facing the consequences of past actions which can bring some level of suffering, **we also have full control in how we respond**

to this suffering. We can choose to resist, be consumed by negativity and potentially add to future karmic burdens, or we can seek the lessons found within suffering, triggering transformative self-growth and future positive karmic cycles.

Other Spiritual Traditions

Buddhism, emerging around the 6th century BCE, inherited the concept of karma but significantly transformed its framework. The Buddhist perspective is consistent with the understanding of karma as energy, inertia, and cause-effect dynamics. However, while the cycle of Samsara and the Law of Cause and Effect were accepted, the Buddha emphasized that there was no fixed, unchanging "soul" that transmigrated. Instead, the idea of "Anatta," or no-self, suggested a fluid bundle of consciousness and tendencies shaped by actions. By adding the dimension of consciousness, the Buddha emphasized the importance of present-moment choices.

The purpose of the teaching was to shift the focus from passive acceptance of karmic retribution towards proactive transformation of karma with conscious intentions and actions. This underpins the concept of karma as a learning mechanism, echoing the principle of "variety in experience," but shifts the emphasis from mere balancing to the possibility of liberation from the karmic cycle altogether through becoming awake in the present moment (choosing each action with full awareness and not doing things blindly, repeatedly, unendingly).

Jainism, another ancient Indian religion, held a more deterministic view of karma. They believed that past actions materialized as subtle particles that clung to the soul, dictating future circumstances in minute detail. Jain ethics, therefore, emphasized extreme caution and non-harming (ahimsa) to avoid attracting further negative karmic bonds. Liberation was understood as the purification and eventual shedding of all karmic residue.

As these diverse perspectives evolved and intertwined, karma became a central pillar of Indian spiritual philosophy. It offered explanations for the inequalities of life, emphasized personal responsibility, and provided a framework for cultivating righteous behavior.

Outside of India, understandings of karma also began to take root. The core Confucian text, *The Analects*, enshrines the adage "Do not impose on others what you yourself do not desire." Moreover, the concept of filial piety, a cornerstone of Confucian ethics, suggests that acts of respect towards elders generate positive karmic energy that benefits not only the individual but subsequent generations. *Tao Te Ching*, a foundational text of Taoism, speaks of the "Way of Heaven," noting that it "benefits and does not harm" and "acts without striving." This points to a natural order where actions in alignment with the Tao yield balance, while disruptions and selfish pursuits lead to disharmony.

The *Kojiki*, an ancient chronicle of Japanese Shinto myths, highlights the concept of "tsumi" — impurities that defile individuals and bring about misfortune. Shinto purification rituals (harai, misogi) embody the importance of cleansing oneself of *tsumi* to restore personal and communal harmony, reflecting a desire to rectify the effects of past actions that violate the cosmic balance. The adage "you reap what you sow" or the idea that "what goes around comes around" are echoes of the universal Law of Karma, although stripped of its spiritual context.

In recent centuries, Western societies saw the introduction of the concept of karma into New Age movements of the nineteenth and twentieth centuries. However, interpretations were often simplified and sometimes fatalistic, overlooking the complexity and emphasis on personal agency found in its original context.

Understanding karma's historical origins is crucial to avoid misinterpretation and appreciate its depth. Being far more than a simplistic system of rewards and punishments, karma embodies the interconnectedness of existence, the potential for self-transformation, and the invitation to act from a place of conscious intention.

So far, we have reviewed the broad strokes of the key purpose of karma and how it functions, tracing its spiritual evolution throughout the years across different religious and spiritual traditions — including even from a scientific perspective. The next section now zooms in and examines the 8 foundational laws of karma. Collectively, these laws reflect the entire and complete working of karma, explaining and shedding logical light on why karma functions the way it does.

Part 2

The 8 Laws of Karma

1st Law of Karma: Oneness

The Grand Law of Karma is built on the most fundamental spiritual truth of all existence — that of Oneness. The veil of separation that we have agreed to temporarily experience as part of this reality on Earth creates the illusion that each of us is isolated and individual beings are disconnected from one another. However, at the highest level of consciousness, reality is profoundly interconnected. In fact, we are not only interconnected, but inextricably a part of a singular, vast, Divine Source. This Oneness is the very fabric of reality, the infinite field of consciousness from which everything manifests.

> *"That which is the finest essence — this whole world has that as its soul. That is Reality. That is the Self. That thou art."* — *Chandogya Upanishad 6.8.7*

> *"In the sky, there is no distinction of east and west; people create distinctions out of their own minds and then believe them to be true."* — *The Buddha*

This understanding unlocks an irrevocable shift in our comprehension of karma. When we recognize the truth of Oneness, the idea of "actions on others" transforms radically. To harm anything or anyone in the universe is to, quite literally, harm ourselves. Every act of cruelty, every intention born of malice, ripples through this unified field, returning eventually to its Creator. We become not only victims of our own negativity but also perpetrators against the ***very essence of our being***. Conversely, acts of love, compassion, and service uplift not only the recipient but also the giver, for they vibrate in harmony with the fundamental nature of the universe.

The entire universe — this infinite field of consciousness — is not a passive backdrop. It is an intelligent, living matrix that records the subtle imprint of every intention, thought, word, and deed. This is referred to as the Akashic Records, a cosmic "library" that stores the journey of every soul. Nothing escapes this accounting, no matter how fleeting or seemingly insignificant. The profound truth spoken by Christ — "for with the measure you use, it will be measured to you (Luke 6:38)" — reveals the universe as an incorruptible system ensuring profound accountability. Every intention or action, even in its most minute details, is recorded forever within the infinite field of consciousness. As Master David Hawkins similarly ascertains in his scientific research on enlightenment, it is confirmable (at consciousness level 1000) that everyone, without exception, is accountable to the universe.

This understanding of Oneness doesn't absolve us of personal accountability. Instead, it empowers us, for it reveals that our actions have a reach far beyond what we can immediately perceive. When we injure another, we fracture the wholeness within ourselves; similarly, each act of generosity becomes a balm for the wounds of the world AND our own spirit. This offers a potent motivation for choosing actions rooted in love and awareness.

Group Karma

If individual actions reverberate on this cosmic scale, how much greater are the implications of collective action? Group karma is the sum total of the energies generated by a collective identity, an ethnicity, a nation, or even humanity as a whole. Group karma is the collective result of the actions, thoughts, and feelings of a group of people who share a common identity or destiny. Group karma affects and connects all the members of the group, as well as the group as a whole.

Group karma is created by various types of groups, such as families, communities, nations, religions, races and cultures (for example, Christians globally, a national army, and even a neighborhood community are all considered karmic groups). These groups can be cohesive enough to function as a unit and develop their own energetic astral body, which is the subtle energy field where all karma is stored. This causal body of a group contains the impressions, tendencies, and habits that the group has acquired through its actions, thoughts, and feelings in its current and previous incarnations. This energy body then influences the nature of the group's experiences and challenges as well as the group's potential and destiny. Group karma is modified by various factors, such as the free will and responsibility of each member. Individuals who take responsibility and practice accountability can help the collective purify and transcend its group karma.

Wars, acts of oppression, widespread greed, or alternatively, collective movements of compassion and spiritual awakening leave their mark on the world and its inhabitants. As members of different communities and groups, we are bound to the karmic destiny we co-create, whether we consciously participate or not. This underscores our important responsibility not only for our own actions but also for the direction in which we collectively steer our communities.

Family Karma

Family karma is a particular kind of group karma that is common in society. Family karma, also known as generational curses, refers to the burdens and issues that are passed down through a family lineage. These karmic patterns repeat themselves across generations until someone in the family line breaks the cycle and releases the stuck energy.

Examples of family karma include:

- Fears and limiting beliefs, such as a scarcity mindset or fear of poverty
- Patterns of violence or abuse
- Unbalanced sexual energy or dysfunctional relationship patterns
- Negative traditions or cultural beliefs
- Chronic illnesses or health issues

These karmic burdens are often absorbed by children through their upbringing and even through their genetic inheritance. They continue to manifest in each generation until a family member takes responsibility for their own personal growth and healing.

To unwind the energy of family karma, an individual must focus on their own spiritual and emotional development. By setting themselves free from the inherited burdens and traumas, they open up an energetic pathway for other family members to follow.

For instance, if a child grows up in poverty and adopts a scarcity mindset, they can choose to heal those wounds, raise their consciousness, and create a life of abundance by pursuing their dreams. This act of personal transformation not only frees them from the family karma but also makes it easier for other relatives to break out of the cycle of lack.

As more individuals in a family line do the work of releasing old patterns and traumas, the collective energy of the lineage begins to shift. Over time, the family karma can be completely transmuted, allowing future generations to inherit a legacy of healing and empowerment instead of unresolved wounds.

In this way, the healing of family karma is a microcosm of the transformation that is possible on a global scale. As more people do the inner work of releasing inherited burdens and embodying their highest potential, they pave the way for the entire human family to transcend its past and create a future of greater wisdom, love, and unity.

Ultimately, the Law of Karma, with its foundation in Oneness, transcends mere punishment and reward. It is a push for extreme, **radical** self-accountability. We are prompted to look beyond the surface of our actions and dive into the depths of our motivations. Did we help because we genuinely cared, or was it a veiled attempt to gain recognition? Did we lash out in anger born of our own unhealed wounds? This honest introspection is the biggest step one can take towards disentangling ourselves from karmic knots and redirecting our energies towards a higher path.

When we embrace the truth of Oneness, the concept of forgiveness also takes on deeper meaning. To truly forgive another is not simply to absolve them. It's a recognition that ultimately, any harm they've caused is a **reflection of their own fragmented state, a wound within the collective consciousness to which we are all inextricably linked**. Forgiveness, therefore, becomes an act of profound healing as it restores a measure of wholeness not only within the relationship but also within greater existence.

Living in alignment within the framework of Oneness and Law of Karma demands a continuous refinement of our awareness. Spiritual practices like meditation and mindfulness help us tune into the subtle energies and intentions underlying our actions. Through self-observation, we can begin to detect the seeds of negativity before they blossom into destructive acts and consciously sow intentions of love and compassion instead. This conscious co-creation with the universe allows us to not only mitigate the effects of past karma but also shape a future of greater harmony within ourselves and the world around us.

Karma From Eating Meat

Finally, there are karmic repercussions to eating animals, though on a lesser scale than harm caused to other human beings. Animals, while not as spiritually developed as humans, still have a rudimentary consciousness and capacity to suffer. Causing them pain and death for our sustenance still creates conscious suffering that needs to be balanced.

The specific karmic consequences of meat eating will largely manifest as health issues and diseases later in life. This reflects the balancing of the suffering caused.

However, the issue is complex from a spiritual growth perspective. In the early stages of human development, both physically and spiritually, eating some meat is necessary to provide the energy and nutrition required. Vegetarianism in childhood will hinder physical development.

But as one progresses on the spiritual path, the need for meat diminishes. The more spiritually advanced one becomes, the more one naturally gravitates towards a plant-based diet. As the soul matures, it gradually transcends the lower animal nature and develops the higher faculties of compassion, wisdom, and unity consciousness. Eating meat is associated with the lower instincts of predation, aggression and violence. Therefore, voluntarily ceasing to eat meat is an important milestone that indicates spiritual growth and mastery over one's base nature.

That said, even for meat-eaters, the karmic impact can be mitigated by factors like:

- Eating only what is necessary for health, rather than gluttonously
- Showing gratitude and respect for the animal's sacrifice
- Using all parts of the animal rather than wastefully discarding
- Choosing meat from animals that were treated humanely in life

Ultimately, from the highest spiritual perspective, all life is sacred and avoiding meat altogether is considered ideal. However for the majority still on the path of evolution, it is important to reduce meat intake slowly in alignment with one's spiritual growth rather than make abrupt changes that can be detrimental to physical health.

2nd Law of Karma: Eternal

The 2nd Law of Karma points to the enduring nature of karma and its link to the fundamental laws of energy. Foundationally, this law states that the consequences of our actions will eternally persist, impacting our spiritual journey until they are consciously transmuted.

Rooted in the core physics principle and eternal truth that energy cannot be created or destroyed but only transformed, this law highlights how the karmic imprints of our thoughts, words, and deeds are indelibly imprinted onto the universe. They become energetic threads that bind us to the cycles of cause and effect and Samsara, impacting on our spiritual evolution. The consequences of our actions linger until balanced, hindering further spiritual progress. ***Because energy cannot die, nobody can escape karma.***

In this way, karma – particularly negative karma – functions as a spiritual and energetic burden. Every act that causes pain, disharmony, or harm to any living being generates a corresponding negative charge that adheres to the soul. These karmic bonds manifest in various ways. They can be carried as emotional scars that attract repeat experiences, as a tendency to repeat destructive patterns, or even as a sense of spiritual stagnation, perpetuating cycles of suffering until confronted and integrated.

This dense energy acts as an energetic hindrance for the harming soul, for it is literally a burden which the soul carries about. In relation to the ascension process, negative karma acts as a downward pull, keeping the soul anchored to lower vibrational states, opposed to the upward movement towards higher consciousness and spiritual liberation that lies at the heart of ascension. Karma thus represents an energetic binding that holds the soul in bondage to the lower dimensions of experience, countervailing the upward force of ascension and preventing the soul from rising to the higher dimensions of experience.

In order to cut away from the soul the negative energy which resulted from negative action, it is necessary for the soul to pass through an equivalent episode of pain or difficulty. This may not be a direct one-to-one correspondence but can manifest in a variety of equivalent ways. For example, rather than killing someone and needing to be killed in turn, the murderer may choose to come back in another life and dedicate his entire life to serving the person he had wronged before (figuratively, a life for a life). If that can be brought about in the same life or a subsequent one, then the negative karmic consequences of the original act are removed. In order for a soul to continue rising in consciousness, it has to release its accumulated karma.

We Observe Our Own Karma

Recall that in the Creator's eyes, there is no guilt and no sin. His love for all beings and entities is too vast for accusation or condemnation. In fact, there is no "higher judgment by God" in the way that we have been made to believe, and it is actually intended by the Creator for darkness and evil to exist in this world simply to allow different souls to choose different experiences (although there is a difference between choosing to experience a single dark experience vs being unconsciously and repeatedly led into darkness and hence trapped).

Karma arises from ***conscious*** suffering — both by the person being victimized but also by our own conscious self as the agent of action. Thus, it is actually **our own souls** that judge and condemn ourselves, for all men know within the core of their being what constitutes holy action. And each soul writes in his own Akashic Records the details of the acts which are against the laws of creation, love and light.

Generally, we attract our own karma quickly in order to set it aside and grow. As our own observer, this karma is automatic, arising immediately as a consequence of any negative action; and just as automatic is the necessity that any karma of this nature must at some time be set aside through suffering. Usually, the suffering is on the part of the one responsible for the original action, but occasionally, as in the instances of healing by Christ and other lightworkers, some of the burden can assumed by another being.[1]

Karma allows us to learn important lessons, so that we can experience and choose differently. It works in a cyclical manner — for example, one who is cruel to others will, as a result, also suffer cruelty at the hands of others.

This will be repeated endlessly until the person realizes how painful it is to be treated cruelly. Through this understanding, he will seek not to perpetuate it. The karmic cycle is then completed — he has experienced both sides of the coin (treating others and being treated cruelly), has grown in consciousness so much because of this, and can now choose differently because of the lesson learnt.

At the end of the day, the point of karma is for us to really be conscious of our words, thoughts and actions — with the knowledge that we are never "victims" of the world, but are active creators of every situation unfolding in our lives. Know that all situations encountered — especially painful ones — are arranged by none other than our own higher selves for us to experience and learn specific lessons.

Ignorance and Responsibility

The more man knows, the more he is responsible for. The weight of karmic responsibility increases as a person gains a greater understanding of the universe. Thus, a person with a knowledge

---

[1] This is discussed in the 8th Law of Karma.

of spiritual law, which he does not practice, suffers greatly in consequence. "The fear of the Lord (law) is the beginning of wisdom." (Proverbs 9:1.)

Recall that all is one consciousness, and that conscious awareness is necessary for full consequence. At the egoic level within an incarnation, if we are truly ignorant of our actions, this does mean that we would be subject to lesser judgment (by ourselves). Ignorance makes the process of learning a karmic lesson less painful. It offers grace for growth without the additional burden of shame or guilt. **In this way, intention matters.** A person seeking to help — but ending up causing harm — incurs much less karma than a person intending to harm to begin with. However, this does not mean that the karmic consequences are negated, as indeed all actions will generate an opposite and equal reaction. The immediate physical repercussions of an action follow universal laws regardless of our intent; if you punch someone maliciously, they experience pain — and so must you.

However, karmic consequences exist on multiple levels. The long-term, heavier soul-level lessons are amplified when we act with conscious intent to harm, despite knowing the consequences. Karma debt and true spiritual suffering is more severe when tied to conscious wrongdoing. This is where feelings of guilt, restlessness, and a lack of inner peace — all forms of karmic consequence — manifest most strongly.

Just as a child playing with matches causes the same fire as an arsonist but their level of culpable responsibility is matched by their lesser understanding, so too does our level of spiritual awareness directly affect and mitigate our karmic consequences. **Spiritual understanding is never simply an intellectual exercise; the possession of spiritual knowledge demands that we align our actions with the higher principles that we now know.** Knowing better means that we are held to a higher standard, both by our own inner judgment and by the laws of the universe.

Spiritual evolution depends on acting upon this accrued wisdom and knowledge. Refusal to apply that knowledge creates stagnation and an intense inner conflict. Furthermore, inaction when we know the "right" path that we should take is a form of negative karma in itself. This creates a unique energetic debt that manifests as guilt, anxiety, and a sense that we aren't fulfilling our potential, hindering our spiritual evolution.

On the flip side, ignorance is also no excuse. Even when we are genuinely unaware, karma accumulates until the underlying lesson is fully absorbed. It can manifest as recurring negative life patterns, attracting similar painful experiences that will cumulatively force one into a painful realization. Ultimately, soul evolution demands a proactive search for knowledge and the application of that knowledge. Stagnation in ignorance impedes this process.

Time and Karmic Backlash

Finally, even though karma is eternally enduring, the speed in which one receives karmic backlash is generally tied to one's level of consciousness. For a soul of lower consciousness, the consequences of his action may take years or even lifetimes to reverberate back. The slower karmic process allows young souls to learn and integrate lessons at a pace that aligns with their current level of understanding and readiness. If karmic repercussions were to manifest too quickly or intensely for a young soul, it would be overwhelming and hinder their growth. Also, recall that karma is here to allow a wide range of experiences. If one is still choosing darkness, one **must not be hindered** from doing so for at least a reasonable amount of time — and hence the delayed karma.

Conversely, karmic consequences are quickly felt by mature souls determined to make progress. The effects of karma manifest more quickly because they are more capable of understanding and integrating these lessons. Souls of high consciousness also seek out opportunities for spiritual development and are willing to face challenges head-on. This willingness to evolve allows them to move through karmic cycles quickly as they are less resistant to the lessons presented. The universe responds more swiftly to those who are more conscious, providing them with the necessary experiences to continue their growth.

3rd Law of Karma: Neutrality

The 3rd Law of Karma emphasizes its inherent neutrality. Karma is not a system designed for punishment but functions as a cosmic account, recording both positive and negative energetic imprints on the soul.

What Are Positive and Negative Actions?

It is important to understand how this relates to righteousness (positive action) and the law, for what is righteous may be illegal and vice versa. Legal systems are human constructs, designed to enforce societal norms through codified laws. These laws are influenced by cultural, political, and historical contexts, and vary greatly across societies and time periods. More importantly, the law is fallible, and can be politically exploited to protect darkness and suppress the light.

In contrast, righteousness is rooted in universal, timeless principles that transcend human-made laws. It is aligned with the intrinsic moral order of the cosmos pertaining to divine justice or cosmic law. Righteousness is about adhering to the Grand Laws and standards that govern the universe, which are immutable and eternal.

To that end, karma is normatively neutral and balances both positive and negative action. We can accrue both positive and negative karma. When the actions taken by one are nurturing and supportive of others, the karma accumulated would be of the same vibration, coming back to lighten the life and the lives which that individual will be living subsequently. By being generous in the past, you will be in receipt of generosity. Every act of kindness, compassion, and selfless service generates a corresponding positive vibration that serves to balance and uplift our karmic profile.

Positive Karma

This positive karma is known as "merit" or karmic surplus. Acts performed with genuine love and a desire to uplift others create reservoirs of positive energy that can ease burdens, attract supportive circumstances, and generally create a sense of overall well-being in our lives. This explains why deeply selfless and compassionate individuals, despite facing challenges, possess a sense of inner peace and resilience.

In Buddhism, the accumulation of merit (puñña) is a central practice for achieving both favorable rebirths and progress towards liberation. Acts of generosity (dāna), ethical conduct (sīla), and mental cultivation (bhāvanā) are meritorious actions that generate positive karmic seeds. As the Dhammapada states, "If a person performs good deeds, happiness follows them like a shadow that never leaves." This points to the manifestation of positive karma as an uplifting energy and a sense of well-being, attracting favorable life circumstances that can range from health, personal beauty to helpful connections

The notion of earning merit through acts of kindness is also found in many other traditions. Sikhs practice "seva" (selfless service), Hindus engage in "punya" (meritorious works), and in Jewish traditions, there's the concept of "mitzvah" (good deeds). Acts of service performed with love and the pure desire to alleviate suffering create reservoirs of spiritual energy that ultimately circulates back to benefit both oneself and the community.

As mentioned, the inner peace and resilience found in selfless individuals is a testament to this principle. Mother Teresa, in performing her service tirelessly amidst profound suffering, is known for her joy and serenity. Nelson Mandela, enduring great hardship, emerged with a spirit of forgiveness and reconciliation. Indeed, while on one hand positive karma does not by itself allow us to transcend prescribed soul challenges, on the other it confers a certain blessing of inner strength and grace that allows us to weather life's storms with a sense of divine optimism, faith and surrender.

However, it's equally crucial to remember that **even positive karma can still tie us to the cycle of rebirth**. Any act, however well-intentioned, if motivated by the ego and a desire for external recognition and reward, further binds us to the wheel of Samsara. Furthermore, while accumulating good karma through righteous actions can lead to favorable circumstances, it can also become a double-edged sword if not approached with enough spiritual maturity. Material benefits such as wealth, power, and social status, often gained through good karma, can become weaknesses if they foster attachment and ego. These benefits create a false sense of security and self-importance, diverting the individual from the path of spiritual growth. The pursuit of material success can lead to ethical compromises and a focus on external validation, which are contrary to the principles of spiritual liberation.

For instance, a wealthy individual may become attached to their possessions and social status, leading to dark actions driven by greed and fear of loss. This attachment creates negative karma, counteracting the positive karma that initially brought them wealth. The cycle of desire and attachment perpetuates Samsara, trapping the individual in a continuous loop of birth, death, and rebirth. True spiritual liberation comes not from accumulating an excess of "good karma" but from transcending the karmic cycle altogether.

Truly, the principal message is this: in impersonal detachment from the material world lies the key to the non-creation of future karma. Even love must become impersonal love, unattached love, ungrasping love, loving detachment—or else it shall forge new bonds in the future.

Ultimately, the 3rd Law of Karma reminds us that karma is not a moralistic force, judging us as "good" or "bad." Instead, it's a dispassionate and utterly fair reflection of the quality of our actions and intentions. Akin to a farmer sowing seeds in a field, the earth does not favor one type of seed over another. It simply reflects back the nature of what is planted, whether nourishing grains or invasive weeds. It is in a similar manner that the universe, through the Grand Law of Karma, responds to the vibrational quality of what we sow.

4th Law of Karma: Destiny

The 4th Law of Karma explicates the dance between free will and the echoes of past actions that shape our present reality. It explains how the key types of karma — lesser karma and greater karma — contrast with each other and how they interplay with free will to shape our ultimate destinies.

There are two main types of karma. The first type is termed ***lesser karma***. This type of karma is the immediate product of our choices and actions within our current and past lives. These are more immediate, tend to be of a lesser degree and are directly observable: a lie leads to distrust; an act of generosity fosters goodwill; cheating on your partner and having them cheat on you in turn. This aligns directly with the adage of us reaping what we sow.

Lesser karma, stemming from our immediate responses to life's stimuli, is considered "lesser" because it originates from our human, egoic level of consciousness. It arises from the ego-mind and its reactive patterning is rooted in low consciousness impressions, attachments, and limiting beliefs. The ego acts based on its conditioning of likes/dislikes, attraction/aversion, rather than wisdom and transcendent awareness — in other words, karma accumulates when we take "wrongful" action to draw corresponding effects we will inevitably experience. Thus, lesser karma creates binding "knots" to the physical plane of existence, ensnaring us in cyclical patterns of action and reaction.

The example of cheating and being cheated on illustrates this clearly. Acting from a place of ego-driven desire or lust initiates a chain of suffering and entanglement as the violated trust must balance itself through further acts of betrayal. The universe reflects back to us the energies we put forth.

The solution to balancing lesser karma lies in raising our consciousness beyond the ego's divisive perspective. Souls of high consciousness make choices from a space of unity, ethics, and non-attachment. Their actions do not create binding karma but are underpinned by love, compassion and liberating wisdom.

Greater Karma

The other type of karma is called ***greater karma***. Greater karma is far more complex and refers to the deeper, unseen influence that is orchestrated based on what our souls want to learn and experience. It is the script our higher selves have written for ourselves, carrying greater lessons for growth that are not linked to egoic violations. It stems from the higher self's desire to experience a particular lifetime in a specific manner so as to learn specific lessons by undergoing certain experiences and events, and (with the help of others who agree to support our higher self's desire) by operating in a manner that will permit a soul to grow.

Greater karma typically manifests as seemingly pre-determined circumstances we're born into, major life events beyond our obvious control, or deep-seated psychological patterns that profoundly shape our lives. For example, a Master Soul might choose to incarnate into a family where he suffered a childhood accident and subsequently acquired a physical handicap ***not*** because he needed to unwind negative karma, but simply because the soul is in pursuit of mastery and wanted the experience of such a handicap as a challenge to raise its consciousness.

In practice, this kind of karma can be either emotionally or personality-based, as in the case of someone suffering from unconscious phobias and conditions caused by trauma in childhood or originating from physically-based challenges, as in the case of a severe illness.

In this respect, homosexuality can sometimes be a result of greater karma. For example, by choosing an incarnation that will face the natural challenge of societal discrimination, the soul will gain much in fortitude, strength and empathy. Recall that our souls are androgynous in nature (possessing both the divine masculine and feminine) and homosexuality arises more as a natural expression of the Creator, as attempts by souls to correct imbalance in development (such as a soul who had many female incarnations trying a male one, but lapsing back to old tendencies) or as attempts by more advanced souls to transcend the male/female duality in this 3D reality — rather than a karmically negative outcome. Nonetheless, karma can be a factor, such as where a homophobic person takes an incarnation as a homosexual person to unwind accrued karma.

While it may be possible, through faith, forgiveness of self and conscious will, to minimize the effects of greater karma that is emotionally placed, usually greater karma is difficult to escape — although it certainly can be mastered and experienced through the positive pole. But in the extreme, when greater karma is represented through a severe handicap or incurable illness, it is usually something that remains present and is constantly in play throughout the lifetime.

Now it must be understood that everyone has a certain amount of greater karma. It is simply the lessons, the mission, prescribed by your own soul when planning the incarnation. Greater karma can be as simple a goal as accepting yourself during a lifetime of perceived deformity or handicap. Greater karma is agreed to before incarnation as a "curriculum" for one's spiritual growth over many lives and stems from the spirit's desire to evolve and expand its consciousness, rather than from the need to balance negative egoic activity.

Free Will and Destiny

The interplay between karma, destiny, and free will is thus complex and intricate. While karma — both lesser but also particularly greater karma — sets the stage for our life experiences and presents us with challenges and opportunities, it is our free will that ultimately determines how we navigate and respond to these circumstances.

At the core of this interplay is the recognition that our past actions, thoughts, and intentions have ***already*** woven the karmic threads that shape our current reality. Yet, it is within this karmic framework that our free will comes into play, allowing us to make conscious choices that can either reinforce these existing karmic patterns, worsen them, or transcend them altogether.

With every thought, word, and deed, we have the opportunity to co-create the unfoldment of our divine plan, either reinforcing the karmic knots of the past or untangling them through love and mindful, selfless action.

Consider, for example, two individuals born into similar circumstances of poverty and hardship, a manifestation of their past karmic burdens. One individual might succumb to despair and resentment, further solidifying negative patterns and accumulating more karmic debt. The other, however, might find within these challenges an ignition of compassion, resilience, and an unwavering determination to transcend their circumstances, leading to transformative personal growth and the creation of positive karma.

As we become more aware of the karmic forces at play in our lives, we gain the power to make conscious choices that align with our highest path. Through introspection and a mindful awareness of our present actions, we can gain insights into our recurring patterns and tendencies brought about by both lesser and greater karma. Armed with this awareness, we can consciously make better choices, reducing the accumulation of further karmic knots and gradually untangling the threads of past karma.

Remember that karma is not a divine punishment or a fatalistic force but rather a universal principle of cause and effect — one that allows us to experience both sides of the coin, gain wisdom, and ultimately choose differently through the exercise of our free will. Just because we have chosen a certain negative way out of ignorance previously does not mean we have to make the same choice again.

5th Law of Karma: Duty

The 5th Law of Karma, Duty, is rooted in the concept of righteous living and the fulfilment of one's sacred duty or dharma. Dharma refers to the destined duties and responsibilities that a soul needs to undertake – sometimes at the cost of its own karma – in order to contribute to the proper divine functioning of the universe. In very practical terms, this means that we sometimes have to take on "fated" roles of darkness (our duty) in order that others can learn lessons or obtain desired experiences.

We are all asked to align our actions with the eternal dharma, the universal order that sustains all of existence. The Law of Duty reminds us that our actions carry immense weight, not only in shaping our own personal destinies but also in contributing to the greater harmony, function and balance of the universe. By acting in accordance with our dharma, we move in harmony with cosmic rhythm, proactively shaping our karmic journey and lessening the accumulation of further negative karma.

Indeed, our dharma demands that at times it may be necessary for us to create karma for ourselves and others as means of facilitating learning – to act as the antagonist in the soul plan for others. This is exemplified in the Hindu scripture *Bhagavad Gita,* which features a dialogue between Arjuna (representative of a human soul) and Krishna (incarnate of Divinity). Arjuna is faced with a dilemma: he has to fight in a war against his own relatives and friends, who have usurped his kingdom and oppressed his people. He is confused and conflicted about his duty and his karma.

Krishna distinguishes between karma, the chain of actions and consequences, and dharma, the righteous path aligned with cosmic order. While trying to avoid negative karma might involve avoiding war, fulfilling one's dharma as a warrior prince who will liberate his people overrides the seeming karmic consequences. Krishna emphasizes that inaction in the face of injustice would violate Arjuna's dharma and actually incur negative karma. Krishna urges Arjuna to see beyond his personal relationships and attachments.

The relatives on the opposing side are merely temporary roles in the eternal dance of life. Focusing on the broader good and upholding dharma takes precedence over individual emotions. Ultimately, Krishna reveals the universe as a divine play, where all roles, even seemingly cruel ones, are part of a cosmic dance. Accepting this perspective allows Arjuna to see the war as an extension of the divine will, further reducing his personal responsibility and guilt.

A similar scenario played out in the events of World War II, where European nations chose the appeasement route against Hitler contrary to righteous dharma, which demanded resistance towards Hitler's actions which were threatening a large number of people, communities and countries.

Another related scenario could be seen when a person works in a company that ends up harming society (pesticides, harmful vaccines etc.), or when one is tasked with duties such as participating in war or state-sanctioned executions. While the act itself may be in karmic violation at the highest level, the extent of karmic culpability depends on the motive and inner state of each person. If we participate reluctantly out of obligation, without cruel intent, we incur less karma. However, if we take satisfaction in cruelty, aligning psychologically with the act, then this will generate greater consequences.

The degree of guilt is proportional to our awareness of the moral wrong and our level of active participation. In such cases, the key to reducing karma is to act with impersonal detachment, performing one's duty without attachment to the fruits of the action (discussed further below in Karma Yoga). It is not just the action itself, but the inner state and motive of the individual, that determines karmic repercussions. Social practices may be wrong — and ideally one should detach themselves entirely from the situation — but if unavoidable out of duty or circumstances, then each person's level of karmic responsibility depends on their own relationship to the act.

Ultimately, our dharma is not merely a personal endeavor but a sacred responsibility that ripples outward, influencing the collective universal plan of humanity. Each act of selfless service, performed with the utmost integrity and dedication, contributes to the harmonious unfolding of the divine plan, allowing us to play our key roles and co-create the grand tapestry of existence.

Just as Arjuna wrestles with his duty on the battlefield, we face our own inner conflicts when making choices. Krishna's guidance reminds us that even amidst karmic consequences, true choice lies in our action. Liberation does not lie in the renunciation of action but in the selfless dedication to our ***righteous duties***.

Karma Yoga: The Path of Action

Karma Yoga, a cornerstone philosophy within the *Bhagavad Gita*, similarly transcends the simplistic notion of karma being merely about "doing good deeds." It's a spiritual path that utilizes action itself as a tool for liberation from the cycle of karma and the limitations of the ego. Recall that within the cycle of Samsara, we accumulate karma based on our actions, desires, and intentions. Every choice we make, conscious or unconscious, leaves an imprint that shapes our future experiences.

Traditionally, inaction (sannyasa) has been considered a path to liberation — the logic is that if we do not act, it is then impossible to accumulate karma! However, Karma Yoga challenges this notion by highlighting the dangers of inaction fueled by fear or escapism. It emphasizes the importance of performing our inherent duties (dharma) without getting entangled in the web of desires for results (phala). By calling on us to perform our required roles with a sense of detached engagement, Karma Yoga shifts the focus from an egoic desire to achieve a specific outcome (not accumulate karma) towards **fulfilling our sacred duty** with integrity and awareness.

Consider the example of the selfless teacher, one who pours their heart into educating students. Their motivation is not driven by a desire for praise or recognition, but by a genuine passion for awakening young minds. Even if some students struggle, the teacher continues their duty with dedication. Similarly, an artist practicing Karma Yoga creates art driven by their inner vision and a desire for self-expression, not seeking fame or fortune. **The action itself becomes a form of divine expression**. They wouldn't be discouraged by a lack of initial recognition, remaining focused on their artistic integrity.

By consistently acting with detached engagement, profound transformations occur: the ego's cravings for external validation and control diminish, allowing inner peace to take root. Actions performed without attachment also leave a lighter karmic residue. Over time, the consistent practice of Karma Yoga weakens the hold of karma, leading to liberation. Finally, when we act in service to a higher purpose and without personal motives, we align ourselves with the divine flow of energy and gain a deeper sense of purpose.

It's important to understand that Karma Yoga and the Law of Duty does not advocate for mindless action. The *Bhagavad Gita* emphasizes the importance of combining action with knowledge and wisdom (Jnana) in order to act consciously.

Violence versus Non-Violence?

Karma Yoga presents an interesting contradiction from the perspective of duty and action advocated by Jainism, which mandates absolute non-harm towards any living being, even in the most minute forms. Recall that the Jain path to liberation emphasizes minimizing actions that accrue negative karma (especially violence), advocating for asceticism and an eventual complete cessation of action.

On the flipside, Karma Yoga recognizes the innate need for human action within the world, emphasizing individual dharma and duty rather than advocating universal asceticism. It offers a path to those bound by worldly duties, allowing engagement in society, fulfilling family roles, or protecting others — all while maintaining internal detachment to avoid being entangled by results-oriented action.

To illustrate this, let us consider the example of a murderer on his way to a mass shooting in a school. Strict Jainist ahimsa would forbid any intervention, while Karma Yoga would call for righteous intervention in such an extreme situation. The emphasis on duty (dharma) would justify stopping (and potentially hurting) the murderer to protect the innocent, recognizing that while this action causes harm to the murderer, inaction would lead to even greater harm.

Thus, Karma Yoga navigates this duality, offering a karmic framework for those engaged in worldly life. It represents an approach of wisdom and nuance, particularly for those living in the complexities of society. Jainism's extreme focus on non-harm can lead to paralysis in the face of injustice or extreme danger.

6th Law of Karma: Relief

Relief, the 6th Law of Karma, addresses a common misconception surrounding the Law of Karma. This Law of Relief reminds us that far from condoning indifference, the true essence of karmic wisdom compels us to alleviate suffering whenever and wherever possible. It teaches that **the act of refusing to help those in need is itself a karmic action that carries significant consequences**. By turning a blind eye to the struggles of others, we become complicit in perpetuating suffering and entangle ourselves in the very karmic web we sought to avoid.

This law emphasizes that compassion and active service are not only virtuous but essential to our collective spiritual evolution. It reminds us that we are all interconnected, and the suffering of one is ultimately the suffering of all. By extending a helping hand, we not only fulfil our sacred duty to assist those in need but also contribute to the collective uplifting of consciousness.

The path of a soul may involve hardships chosen for specific lessons and growth opportunities, even if we observers from the outside struggle to comprehend why. This lack of understanding shouldn't negate our responsibility to alleviate suffering where possible. While a soul's journey is their own, offering support and kindness remains a vital part of our spiritual practice.

A Fallen Interpretation

Throughout history, many, especially in the great Eastern cultures and traditions, have misconstrued the Grand Law of Karma to mean that one should not interfere with the karmic destiny of another, either to hinder or to help him in his endeavors. They have interpreted the Law of Karma as justification for inaction in the face of suffering.

This has been a grievous error in understanding, for it has allowed a continuation of suffering where this might have been alleviated. The very action of refusing to help in such circumstances brings its own karmic consequences upon the person refusing.

Early in the Christian era, elders of the Christian movement pondered whether to teach the ancient truths of karma and rebirth to the members of the fledgling Christian movement. After much debate, Church elders decided to exclude these teachings. The reason was their observation of this interpretative error into which the people of the East had fallen.

This is why the Christian teaching emphasizes, above all else, the commandment to serve one's brother in any way possible. For through this service, it is possible not only to set aside one's own karmic burden, but to lift the load from the shoulders of another. Christ, who came to show the way for the Piscean Age, spent much of His time lifting the burdens from others. He healed the sick; He fed the hungry; He helped all who came to seek His aid.

Christ's teachings emphasized the profound importance of easing the suffering of others. Compassionate action – ***and this is very importantly differentiated from unwelcomed intervention or self-sacrificial action*** – not only breaks karmic cycles for those involved but also generates positive karma for the giver, creating a ripple effect of positive energy. By approaching those who suffer with a spirit of understanding and offering help, we plant seeds of transformation within their hearts, offering a path of redemption to even those bound by negative karmic patterns.

It is not for man to know the extent of his own karma or that of others. Restricted by our narrow consciousness and the limitations of three-dimensional existence, we cannot hope to know all of the intricate complexities of the karmic patterns that have been created by man's actions. It is best for us simply to trust that karma will work itself out to the benefit of all souls, and to occupy ourselves with service to our brothers.

Ultimately, our actions impact not just our own karmic trajectories but also across the human experience in its totality. By actively working to alleviate suffering and offering mercy, we become the vessel of divine grace, embodying principles that unwind and break cycles of karmic entanglement.

7th Law of Karma: Forgiveness

Having accrued karmic debt – as all of us have at different points in time – what are we then to do? **The key to karmic relief is forgiveness.** Within the dynamics of the Grand Law of Karma, forgiveness stands as one of the most powerful forces of liberation.

True forgiveness, particularly of oneself and others, neutralizes karma rooted in ego-based actions (lesser karma) – those driven by anger, hatred, greed, or a desire to inflict harm. This shift in consciousness lessens the magnetic pull that will attract negative experiences to those entangled in that karmic pattern. When forgiveness replaces resentment in this way, the cycle of retribution fueled by the ego is broken.

Forgiveness also releases the heavy emotional burdens associated with past hurts and negative attachments to anger, resentment, and the desire for vengeance. This liberation alters one's vibrational state, influencing future karmic experiences.

However, it is important to understand that forgiveness is not a complete erasure of the involved karmic debt – but a transformation of it. Recall that karma, at its core, is about learning and growth. Forgiveness doesn't eliminate the consequences of past actions but will ***change how these consequences manifest in our lives.*** Instead of harsh or painful experiences commensurate with spiraling levels of hurt and retribution, karmic repercussions will shift towards opportunities for learning the lessons of compassion, empathy and understanding.

Forgiveness is primarily an internal transformation. Even if external circumstances don't change immediately, cultivating forgiveness lessens the inner turmoil experienced. The consequences of our past actions will still manifest, but with forgiveness we face them with greater strength, wisdom, and a less reactive emotional state.

Think of forgiveness like this. With karmic debt representing a negative energetic entanglement to another person, embracing true forgiveness will move to sever the ties of negativity — although the consequences of the initial actions still need to be unwound to achieve balance.

True forgiveness doesn't mean condoning another's actions or denying your own hurt. It means letting go of the desire for revenge or clinging to the role of victim by taking co-creative responsibility for what had happened and understanding its greater lessons. Remember, everything that happens in your life, good or bad, is a result of choices you have made or the soul agreements your higher self has reached. At no point can your free will ever be violated.

In practice, forgiveness can be achieved through this sequence of actions (useful for both lesser and greater karma from past and present lives):

1. First, understand and completely accept that whatever is being experienced is not random "injustice," but one which you have purposely created for yourself in the grand scheme of things to learn a certain lesson. Accept that whatever is happening is caused by you, and that it has meaning and purpose to it.
2. Meditate and pray on it for its meaning.
3. Make honest acknowledgment of your failure to meet past obligation. Reflect on the lessons you are asked to learn through this experience. Commit to learning this lesson well and never repeating it again on purpose.
4. Having this understanding and acceptance, surrender to the situation. Let go, and let it play out as it is without further reacting negatively to it.
5. Next, express earnest willingness to meet that karma obligation. As much as possible, take appropriate reparative action to alleviate the problem if you are

the perpetuator, including compensation, verbal and emotional acknowledgement. If you are the "victim," it is not necessary to demand these as the universe will equalize all outcomes justly, but make a fair request and allow yourself to receive if offered.

6. Affirm that particular strength the absence of which led to the karma to begin with. For example, if it is a karmic issue of you being cruel in the past, affirm otherwise – that you are compassionate and loving. The use of affirmations, meditation, and prayer, the study of the Scriptures, the practice of the virtues, and the rendering of service to others are very powerful. Nonetheless, genuine growth cannot be mechanically induced. Unless and until one's consciousness has truly risen in love, these practices will not be entirely effective.
7. Lastly, completely embrace forgiveness in this issue. Truly forgive yourself for your role in this situation and forgive the other person both for their role in it, and for reacting and behaving the way they did.

"Father, forgive them; for they do not know what they are doing" (Luke 23:34).

If these steps are sincerely taken at any point in the karmic cycle, it will break and ultimately put a stop to the cycle, lifting the karmic debt off your shoulders. An example of such a closure of a karmic cycle through forgiveness can be seen in a case when all at once, and for no obvious reason, an abusive relationship that has lasted for years — such as a husband and wife who have been pushing the limits of each other's tolerance — suddenly resolves, and the two have no further effect on each other; the parties go their separate ways, having completely released each other.

8th Law of Karma: Grace

The final Law of Karma, the Law of Grace, introduces a transcendent dimension to our understanding of karma. While karma emphasizes the Law of Cause and Effect, grace offers the possibility of entirely overcoming this cycle through unconditional love.

Grace is the foundation of all existence, the very environment within which all life and experiences unfold. It's the loving and supportive fabric of creation itself. It reflects the benevolence of our Creator that supports and uplifts each soul, even amidst challenges and consequences of past actions, and embodies a boundless love from which we can never truly be separated. Grace eternally assures an unwavering spiritual connection within every being, regardless of actions or choices made. No matter how deeply into the dark a soul strays through their choices and actions, they remain constantly held in love, light, and joy, through their intrinsic unity with the Creator.

The Hermetic principle of "As above, so below" sets out that the macrocosm (universe) reflects the microcosm (human). Grace, then, is the cosmic principle of forgiveness and love, mirrored within the human soul as the potential for divine compassion and release from negativity.

This is what Jesus was referring to when he brought the good news (the gospel) that there was a higher law than the Law of Karma — the Law of Grace — which frees man from the Law of Cause and Effect. "In the world ye shall have tribulation, but Christ said: Be of good cheer; I have overcome the world" (John 16:33).

In practical terms, grace can be understood as a soul's "override button." When a person has consciously mastered the karma prescribed by his higher self — when he has created a link between his egoic incarnation and his higher self and has demonstrated mastery of the ego and greater karma associated with a challenge — grace becomes possible. When reached, grace neutralizes the karma, and the person could be said to be in bliss[2].

A Resolved Contradiction

Grace affects karma in various ways. Some traditions, such as Christianity, teach that grace overrides karma, while others such as Hinduism teach that grace complements karma — that the Divine Source has given souls the ability themselves to overcome their own karma through loving action.

Although initially appearing to be conflicting, in truth **there is no contradiction between both perspectives**. Both views of grace — whether it overrides karma or complements it — stem from a fundamental belief in the unconditional love of a higher power. Both perspectives acknowledge the possibility of transcending karmic limitations. Even those emphasizing grace as a "random" stroke of divine intervention require sincere repentance, a shift in behavior and devotion to demonstrate a change of heart.

Indeed, while grace is an eternal constant, free-will action plays a key role in navigating karma and evolving spiritually. Conscious effort is still required to access the transformative potential of grace. As set out above, forgiveness plays a significant role in both understandings of grace. Letting go of self-reproach and releasing the burden of past actions greatly lessens the emotional weight that perpetuates karmic cycles.

Even if grace doesn't entirely negate karmic consequences, it manifests in ways that will ease the journey. This includes increased strength to face challenges, guidance towards wisdom

[2] Relatedly, achieving this state not just for a specific karmic lesson but for the overall soul journey is the goal of all souls, where it achieves complete neutralization of greater karma and reaches a state of grace that propels its return to Source.

and serendipitous encounters with all sorts of resources helpful for learning karmic lessons.

Ultimately, both karma and grace play a role in spiritual evolution: karma provides lessons and consequences, while grace provides the constant assurance of the potential to end suffering and reconnect with our divine core. This unbreakable connection to the source within each entity is exactly what the concepts of the Gnostic Divine Spark, Christ Consciousness and the Buddha-nature refer to.

Bearing the Karma of Others

Finally, Christ is often viewed as the embodiment of divine grace made manifest in the world. His acts of forgiveness and healing are demonstrations of grace at work, offering a transformative power that is capable of relieving burdens and opening pathways beyond the strict accounting of past actions. Yet in truth, such occurrences should be understood as rare exceptions to the norm. The experiences of Christ do not fit fully within the general scheme of the cosmic laws as he had chosen to, through his purity and high consciousness, temporarily suspend them.

It remains enduringly true that the expression "as you sow, so shall you reap" conveys the truth of the karmic requirement decreed from the very beginning of creation, and this law continues in force throughout. However, Christ decided to lift the karmic burdens from the shoulders of certain individuals, in order to demonstrate that such lifting of karma was possible.

Indeed, it is possible for a given quantum of karma of a person to be removed and assumed by another person. In the case of the Christ, He Himself assumed the karma that was at the root of the illness or suffering of different individuals that he had healed and forgiven. Aside from Christ's example, spiritual masters and gurus sometimes take on some of their students' karmic burdens to expedite their spiritual advancement. Similarly in

Mahayana Buddhism, Bodhisattvas embody the principle of karmic transference by postponing their own enlightenment out of compassion to alleviate the suffering of others. We also see this every day in the work of medical personnel, healers and lightworkers, where they absorb a degree of their patients' suffering as part of the healing process.

However, the practice of assuming another's karma is nuanced and complex. It requires immense spiritual strength and purity; otherwise, the helper risks being overwhelmed by negativity themselves. Additionally, it is also important to be conscious of the fact that karma, even if painful, serves as a catalyst for growth. Completely removing someone's karma could hinder this spiritual development. True support often lies in empowering individuals to face their own challenges and offering compassionate love and support as they work through their karma rather than simply entirely absolving them of it.

Artwork that energetically reflects one of the author's visions on karma.

Final Thoughts

As we reach the conclusion of this book, the principles of karma are no longer just abstract concepts. This book has sought to reveal them as living forces shaping our destinies. You now understand that the Grand Law of Karma offers both a challenge and an opportunity. Karma is a literal mirror, reflecting back the consequences of our actions, and a tool for growth as we learn, adapt, and consciously align ourselves with higher principles. The invitation for you now is to move beyond this intellectual knowledge and put it into transformative practice. Begin by observing the undercurrent of karma within your own life. Witness how your thoughts, words, and deeds ripple outwards, shaping your experiences. Take responsibility for all that you are facing in your life – especially painful relationships and experiences. Embrace being conscious in every moment in life, cultivating awareness of the intentions driving your actions. Strive for compassion, seeking to understand that everyone fights their own battles, bound by their own karmic patterns. Choose forgiveness over resentment, for it liberates you from past burdens and breaks the karmic chains of retribution.

Remember, within this cosmic interplay of cause and effect, you have **complete divine agency**. Every act of love, every intention anchored in service, and every conscious effort to break free from old patterns creates an upward spiral. While the journey might not always be easy, the path of awareness and self-transformation empowers you to co-create a destiny infused with greater peace, purpose, and wisdom.

"If you want to know the past, look into your present conditions. If you want to know your future, look into your present actions."
– Padmasambhava, founder of Tibetan Buddhism.

With the truth of karma as your compass, may you step forward in the divine grace of our Creator as you navigate the tides of karma towards the infinite shores of your highest potential.

Om Mani Padme Hum. May the Loving Light of our Creator guide you Home, and I look forward to seeing you on the other side.

Dr Ric Neo

Biography

Dr Ric Neo is a Spiritual Teacher with a decade of practicing occult experience and a deep expertise in a wide range of Western and Eastern esoteric, occult and spiritual arts. His purpose on Earth is to raise the consciousness of society and to assist in the awakening of those who are ready. He ministers daily online on enlightenment and Higher Spirituality to a global audience (www.x.com/neospirituality).

Dr Neo also operates NeoSpirituality, a spiritual consultancy where he works with clients and students using an integrated East–West and Yin–Yang approach.

Dr Neo has a PhD in Political Science from the University of Hong Kong. He has published widely in the scholarly field of disinformation. Before he decided to pursue the spiritual arts full-time, he was a Professor at a University.

MANTRA
BOOKS

EASTERN RELIGION & PHILOSOPHY

We publish books on Eastern religions and philosophies.
Books that aim to inform and explore the various traditions
that began in the East and have migrated West.
If you have enjoyed this book, why not tell other readers by
posting a review on your preferred book site.

Recent bestsellers from MANTRA BOOKS are:

The Way Things Are

A Living Approach to Buddhism

Lama Ole Nydahl

An introduction to the teachings of the Buddha, and how to make use of these teachings in everyday life.

Paperback: 978-1-84694-042-2 ebook: 978-1-78099-845-9

Back to the Truth

5000 Years of Advaita

Dennis Waite

A demystifying guide to Advaita for both those new to, and those familiar with this ancient, non-dualist philosophy from India.

Paperback: 978-1-90504-761-1 ebook: 978-184694-624-0

Shinto: A celebration of Life

Aidan Rankin

Introducing a gentle but powerful spiritual pathway reconnecting humanity with Great Nature and affirming all aspects of life.

Paperback: 978-1-84694-438-3 ebook: 978-1-84694-738-4

In the Light of Meditation

Mike George

A comprehensive introduction to the practice of meditation and the spiritual principles behind it. A 10 lesson meditation programme with CD and internet support.

Paperback: 978-1-90381-661-5

A Path of Joy

Popping into Freedom

Paramananda Ishaya

A simple and joyful path to spiritual enlightenment.

Paperback: 978-1-78279-323-6 ebook: 978-1-78279-322-9

The Less Dust the More Trust

Participating in The Shamatha Project, Meditation and Science

Adeline van Waning, MD PhD

The inside-story of a woman participating in frontline meditation research, exploring the interfaces of mind-practice, science and psychology.

Paperback: 978-1-78099-948-7 ebook: 978-1-78279-657-2

I Know How To Live, I Know How To Die

The Teachings of Dadi Janki: A warm, radical, and life-affirming view of who we are, where we come from, and what time is calling us to do

Neville Hodgkinson

Life and death are explored in the context of frontier science and deep soul awareness.

Paperback: 978-1-78535-013-9 ebook: 978-1-78535-014-6

Living Jainism

An Ethical Science

Aidan Rankin, Kanti V. Mardia

A radical new perspective on science rooted in intuitive awareness and deductive reasoning.

Paperback: 978-1-78099-912-8 ebook: 978-1-78099-911-1

Ordinary Women, Extraordinary Wisdom

The Feminine Face of Awakening

Rita Marie Robinson

A collection of intimate conversations with female spiritual teachers who live like ordinary women, but are engaged with their true natures.

Paperback: 978-1-84694-068-2 ebook: 978-1-78099-908-1

The Way of Nothing

Nothing in the Way

Paramananda Ishaya

A fresh and light-hearted exploration of the amazing reality of nothingness.

Paperback: 978-1-78279-307-6 ebook: 978-1-78099-840-4

Readers of ebooks can buy or view any of these bestsellers by clicking on the live link in the title. Most titles are published in paperback and as an ebook. Paperbacks are available in traditional bookshops. Both print and ebook formats are available online.

Find more titles and sign up to our readers' newsletter at www.collectiveinkbooks.com/mind-body-spirit. Follow us on Facebook at facebook.com/OBooks and Twitter at twitter.com/obooks